TRAVEL DAMAGES

by Alan Saggerson, BCL, MA (Oxon), Barrister

© Alan Saggerson 1998

Published by CLT Professional Publishing
A Division of Central Law Training Ltd
Wrens Court
52-54 Victoria Road
Sutton Coldfield
Birmingham
B72 1SX

ISBN 1 85811 172 2

Typeset by Cheryl Zimmerman
Printed in Great Britain by Ipswich Book Company Limited

To Margaret Saggerson

CONTENTS

PREFACE

[There is] *"a growing belief that every misfortune must, in pecuniary terms at any rate, be laid at someone else's door, and after every mishap, every tragedy, the cupped palms are outstretched for the solace of monetary compensation ..."*

So Mr Justice Rougier is reported as having said in a case forming part of the consolidated appeals in *Capital Counties plc* v *Hampshire* [1997] 3 WLR 331. In the absence of significant personal injury it might be going too far to describe run of the mill holiday and travel complaints as "tragedies" but there can be no doubt that they are "mishaps" in respect of which compensation is claimed (and secured) with ever-increasing regularity. Few causes of action seem to raise the degree of animosity that is encountered in travel cases where arrangements go wrong. Even claims for £150.00 reach the Court of Appeal (*Williams* v *Travel Promotions Limited* [1998] *The Times* 153). The assessment of damages in travel cases is still a relatively new discipline. Decisions can be inconsistent and sometimes even appear unprincipled. It is hoped that this book might help some of those seeking assistance.

This book is only intended as a quick reference guide for those seeking general guidance on the type of damages that may be recoverable. Part 1 deals with holiday and travel cases litigated in the courts of England and Wales, and is concerned mainly with quality and performance complaints. Part 2 is intended as no more than a general introduction to the heads of personal injury damages recoverable in some European jurisdictions (although ultimately there is no substitute for detailed advice from locally qualified experts). No attempt has been made to summarise personal injury damages in the United Kingdom. Some sources of more detailed information have been provided wherever possible.

I am grateful to my colleagues at Barnard's Inn Chambers who have made a number of suggestions and improvements, and to the publishers for their characteristic patience and encouragement. Any errors that remain, are mine. The aim has been to state the law as it was on 30 April 1998.

Alan Saggerson
Barnard's Inn Chambers
Holborn, London, EC1

TABLE OF CASES

TABLE OF STATUTES

TABLE OF
STATUTORY INSTRUMENTS

Part 1

Holiday Claims

HOLIDAY CLAIMS

An overview

Principles   In holiday claims there are four principle heads of damages.

   i   General damages reflecting *loss of bargain*.
   ii General damages compensating for *loss of enjoyment*.
   iii Special damages – expenses and consequential losses.
   iv Damages for injury or illness.

An analysis or recent judicial decisions on quantum in holiday cases is set out at the end of this chapter in Table A. An analysis of special damages awarded in reported cases is set out in Table B. The principles sources for such cases are:

Sources   *Current Law* Monthly and Annual Service
International Travel Law Journal (The Travel Law Centre, University of Northumbria)
Grant & Mason – *Holiday Law* (1995) Sweet & Maxwell
Saggerson – *Travel Law & Litigation* (1996) CLP

Causes of action

Breach of contract (express terms).
Breach of contract (common law implied terms).
Breach of contract (statutory implied terms – the Package Travel etc Regulations 1992 SI 1992 No 3288).
Misrepresentation (fraudulent, negligent or innocent).
Breach of common law duty of care.

Measure of damages

Contract That loss which is such as may fairly and reasonably be considered either as arising naturally from the breach or such as may reasonably be supposed to have been in the contemplation of the parties at the time the contract was made: *Hadley* v *Baxendale* [1854] 9 Exch 341. Such damages are limited to that loss which is reasonably foreseeable, but extend to special losses which should have been in the contemplation of the contract breaker by reason of his actual knowledge at the time the contract was made: *Victoria Laundry (Windsor) Limited* v *Newman Industries Limited* [1949] 2 KB 528.

Tort Such damages as would place the parties in the position they would have enjoyed if the tort had not been committed – or the representation had not been made.

Fraudulent misrepresentation and statutory misrepresentation (section 2(1) Misrepresentation Act 1967)
The general measure of damages in tort plus all consequential losses whether foreseeable or not: *Royscott Trust Limited* v *Rogerson* [1991] 3 All ER 294.

Note   *Chesnau* v *Interholme Limited* [1983] *The Times*, 9 June.
Holiday claim plaintiffs sued in misrepresentation. The county court judge held that if the misrepresentation had not been made they would not have entered into the holiday contract in the first place and would not have incurred the additional expense of alternative accommodation to the proper standard after they arrived at their destination. He awarded them £30.00. The Court of Appeal overturned the award. The judge's approach was unrealistic. The misrepresentation had not been discovered until the plaintiffs arrived. The additional money they spent on proper accommodation was in order to *mitigate* the loss caused by the misrepresentation, and they were entitled to a full recovery. Where a holiday has already commenced before the misrepresentation has been discovered it is artificial to say that in the absence of the representation the parties would have stayed at home and thus not have incurred extra expenditure.

Loss of holiday

Claims against an independent tortfeasor for the loss of a holiday caused by a pre-holiday tort are measured on an entirely separate basis: *Ichard* v *Frangoulis* [1977] 1 WLR 556.

Peter Pain J: "Where a holiday is ruined as a result of an accident, the loss is not measured – *as a separate head of damage but as one of the factors to be taken into account when assessing general damages, and as a factor which would lead me to give rather more by way of general damages than I otherwise would do."*

However, where the ruined holiday represents the greater part of the loss occasioned by an unrelated tortfeasor damages may be calculated on the conventional "holiday" basis: *Graham* v *Kelly & East Surrey NHS Trust [No 2]* (1997) 12 CL 151. In this case a family was compensated for diminution in value and loss of enjoyment where a holiday was taken but significantly compromised as a result of an earlier but unrelated breach of duty by the defendants.

Pleading   It is recommended that all heads of loss are specifically pleaded in holiday claims – including loss of bargain and loss of enjoyment in order to highlight the distinction between them.

HOLIDAY CLAIMS

Loss of bargain

Principle   The difference between what the consumer bought and what was supplied.

Sometimes referred to as "diminution in value" or "difference in value".

In assessing the value of what the consumer bought, reference should be made to the full price irrespective of discounts and special offers – so, *e.g.* where a consumer buys a holiday worth £1,000.00 for £750.00 what he has bought is a £1,000.00 holiday. If what he gets is assessed to be worth only £500.00 the consumer's measure of damages under this head should be £500.00, not £250.00.

Loss of bargain covers the failure to provide what was promised *and* the provision of promised items at a lower *standard* than promised.

Loss of bargain also includes an element for *physical discomfort* (as distinct from impaired enjoyment or distress): *Bailey* v *Bullock* [1950] 2 All ER 1167.

Examples   *Jackson* v *Horizon Holidays* [1975] 3 All ER 92.
Per Lord Denning MR:
"The judge took the cost of the holiday at £1,200.00. The family only had about half the value of it. Divide it by two and you get £600.00."
See also cases digested in Table A.

Calculation   **1. An arithmetical approach**
Where a consumer is accommodated in a two star hotel instead of the five star hotel promised, it may be relatively

straightforward to discover the difference between the cost of the two hotels over the period of the holiday and award the difference under this head. A similar approach may be justified where certain specific facilities are unavailable for an identifiable period of time, or the consumer's arrival is delayed by a given period.

2. A more subjective approach

Usually the arithmetical approach will not be appropriate. The consumer may be accommodated in his chosen hotel but have a variety of "quality" and facility complaints. Assessing the difference in value between a sub-standard or partly sub-standard five star hotel and one of a proper standard is a matter of judgment.

Rules of thumb?

Table A reveals that there is no judicially recognised rule of thumb or starting point for this calculation. However, rounded percentages or figures are often adopted. The following guidance is tentatively suggested.

	Holiday description	*Suggested % of cost*
(i)	Cancelled holiday before or shortly after departure	100%
(ii)	"Grim" – to the point where whole point of the holiday compromised	80% – 90%
(iii)	"Poor" where many facilities and services are manifestly lower quality than promised	70% – 80%
(iv)	"Unsatisfactory" where many facilities and services are lower quality than promised	50% – 70%
(v)	"Standard failures" where some facilities or services are not as promised	up to 50%

The recovery of 100% of the price of the holiday *under this head* is unusual and only arises in cases where there has been a *total failure* of consideration. Even where the facilities provided are poor, the supplier can often show that the consumer got *something* for the price of the holiday even if it fell well below the standard bargained for.

Individual bargains

Some facilities and services are important to *all consumers*: *e.g.* standards of safety, hygiene and cleanliness.
Others are important or of greater importance to *individual consumers*: *e.g.* Sports facilities, tuition, excursions, childrens' services.

When assessing the loss of bargain in individual cases the following items can be used as an initial check-list.

- What facilities and services were included in the contract of general availability? (*e.g.* restaurants, sports, pools, location). Which were not provided?
- What facilities and services were specific to the individual consumer? (*e.g.* type of room, room facilities, meals plan, transport). Which were not provided?
- Over what period of time or proportion of the contract were promised facilities or services unavailable?
- Of both the general and specific facilities and services that *were* provided how does their *standard* compare with what was promised?
- For how long or for what proportion of the contract were the promised facilities sub-standard?
- Which of the missing or sub-standard facilities and services:
  would definitely have been used
  would probably have been used
  might have been used
  by the particular consumer, and to what extent?

Illustration   If a keen scuba diver embarks on a holiday to a resort which promotes its water sports facilities and equipment, the failure to provide advertised scuba facilities, tuition, trips and equipment could seriously impact on the bargain made.

The bargain made by a consumer who wanted to take a beginner's scuba course might be less seriously effected. The bargain of one who had not finally decided whether to use the facilities or not (but was robbed of the opportunity) will be less seriously affected still.

The bargain of the consumer who chose the resort for its location and restaurants should not recover much (if anything) for this failure by the supplier.

HOLIDAY CLAIMS

Loss of enjoyment

Principle   Damages for loss of enjoyment should be distinguished from that element of the *loss of bargain* measured by the discomfort and physical inconvenience of the consumer. Loss of enjoyment is sometimes described by terms such as: vexation; annoyance; frustration and anxiety.

In a proper case, including a contract for a holiday, damages can be recovered for mental distress and vexation. The contract is one for the provision of entertainment and enjoyment: *Jarvis* v *Swan Tours* [1973] QB 233 at 236H – 237A.

Per Edmund Davies LJ at 239G:
"When a man had paid for and properly expects an invigorating and amusing holiday and, through no fault of his, returns home dejected because his expectations have been largely unfulfilled, in my judgment it would be quite wrong to say that his disappointment must find no reflection in the damages to be awarded."

See also *Hayes* v *Dodd* [1990] 2 All ER 815 CA where it was recognised that loss of enjoyment damages were classically recoverable in holiday cases whatever the restrictions on their recovery in other contract situations.

Example   In *Jarvis* (above) the consumer had been accommodated in perfectly satisfactory conditions, but the absence of the promised *après-ski* seriously limited his enjoyment. The Court of Appeal awarded him the equivalent of *double* the cost of the holiday in substitution of the trial judge's award of *half*. This classic case is a good illustration of how the cost of the holiday need not represent the ceiling of a possible award when loss of bargain and loss of enjoyment are added together – even where the consumer gets something for his money.

Calculation   Column 6 of Table A shows the evolution of this head of damage as a separate item in recent years and the amounts in proportion to the total cost of a holiday that loss of enjoyment often represents. It will be seen that the proportion differs considerably from case to case. It is not surprising that such a subjective head of damage should be closely linked to the distinctive facts of individual cases.

"... in this kind of case it is even more difficult than in a personal injuries case to arrive at the appropriate figure with any degree of precision." (Bridge LJ *Adock* v *Blue Sky Holidays* [1980] CA unreported)

Factors   The following factors often have an important bearing on the level of damages for loss of enjoyment:

● The type of holiday – *e.g.* special occasions; weddings; honeymoons; retirement.
● The number of holidays taken by the consumers in question, and the likelihood of them enjoying more holidays in the near future, and/or many in the past.
● The extent of the breaches of contract and their impact on individual consumers – *e.g.* loss of sports facilities for proven sportsman.

Proportionality

There is no general principle articulated in the reported cases to the effect that damages for loss of enjoyment should be proportional to the cost of the holiday. For example, there is no reason in principle why a modestly priced holiday taken by a family in relatively straightened financial circumstances should not lead to loss of enjoyment damages assessed at several times the cost of the holiday – particularly if the consumers could only afford to travel occasionally, or had done so on this occasion, for a particular reason or celebration not likely to recur in the near future.

"There can be no doubt that there is an increasing tendency on the part of ... Judges ... to award damages well in excess of the value of the holiday concerned. A notional ceiling on these damages based on the cost of the holiday can no longer necessarily be assumed ..." (Brown & Stratton: (1997) 4 TLJ 176).

Special features

Even where damages are assessed for breach of contract, the compensator must take his victim as he finds him (*Page* v *Smith* [1995] 2 WLR 644). There are, however, limits on the recoverability of damages where special features *unknown to the organiser* prevail.

- In *Ashcroft* v *Sunset Holidays plc* (reported in *The "Eggshell Personality" and Package Holidays* (1997) TLJ 173) a terminally ill, psychiatrically disturbed holidaymaker lost her claim for damages for a nervous breakdown following a very poor holiday with Sunset. Such dramatic psychiatric consequences were simply not foreseeable, and psychiatric illness of this magnitude resulting from the provision of a sub-standard holiday was not in the contemplation of the parties when the contract was made. Sunset had no knowledge of the plaintiff's mental condition.
- *Kemp* v *Intasun* [1987] FTLR 234 is an earlier example of the same principle. The tour operator was responsible for the foreseeable up-set, distress and anxiety of a dirty hotel room, but not for his personal injury and illness (a severe asthma attack) which was not a foreseeable consequence of being placed in a filthy room – in the absence of special knowledge on the part of the tour organiser.

Accordingly, where there is injury or illness going beyond the realms of what would be ordinarily contemplated as a likely consequence of the breach of contract on the part of the holiday provider, damages are *not* recoverable. However, where *foreseeable* loss of enjoyment, aggravation, vexation and anxiety are simply made worse because of the nature or personality of the claimant, such foreseeable consequences *do* sound in damages.

Table A

Case	Reference	Price	Loss of bargain	% of price	Loss of enjoyment	% of price
Hunt – school trip – children	CLY 1983 – 983	£98.00 each	£60.00 each	61.22%	No separate award	–
Hunt – teachers	CLY 1983 – 983	£98.00 each	£110.00 each	112.24%	No separate award	–
Hunt – lead teacher	CLY 1983 – 983	£98.00	£210.00	214%	No separate award	–
Rhodes – family of 5	CLY 1983 – 984	£777.00	£1,000.00	128.7%	No separate award	–
Taylor – family	CLY 1984 – 1023	£1,306.52	£900.00	70%	£400.00	30.63%
Bagley – single	CLY 1984 – 1024	£642.00	£1,500.00	233.6%	No separate award	–
Abbatt – family of 4	CLY 1984 – 1025	£769.00	£1,000.00	130%	No separate award	–
Scott – couple	CLY 1985 – 943	£512.00	£400.00	78.13%	No separate award	–
Harris – family of 5	CLY 1985 – 944	£1,400.00	£1,000.00	71.43%	No separate award	–
Powell – couple	CLY 1985 – 945	unknown	£750.00	unknown	No separate award	–
Tucker – family of 3	CLY 1986 – 383	£452.62	£129.29	28.56%	£300.00	66.28%
Jacobs – family of 4	CLY 1986 – 975	£2,455.00	£2,455.00 (refunded)	100%	£250.00	10.18%
Carter – family of 5	CLY 1986 – 976	£859.00	£359.00	41.79%	£1,000.00	116.41%
Glover – couple	CLY 1987 – 1151	£2,290.81	£2,290.81	100%	£1,600.00	69.84%
McLeod – family	CLY 1987 – 1162	£1,030.00	£439.00	42.62%	£500.00	48.54%
Duthie – single	CLY 1988 – 1058	unknown	£294.00	unknown	£250.00	unknown
Wilson – school trip	CLY 1988 – 1059	£249.00 each	£125.00	50.20%	No separate award	–
Wilson – teacher	CLY 1988 – 1059	Free	–	–	£200.00	–
Wilson – party leader	CLY 1988 – 1059	Free	–	–	£400.00	–
Jones – family	CLY 1988 – 1061	unknown	£750.00	unknown	£1,000.00	unknown

Case	Reference	Price	Loss of bargain	% of price	Loss of enjoyment	% of price
Graham – family	CLY 1989 – 1189	unknown	–	–	£900.00	unknown
Corbett – couple	CLY 1989 – 1194	£910.00	£711.00	78%	£1,039.00	114.18%
Booth – couple	CLY 1990 – 1542	£584.00	£400.00	68%	£1,200.00	205.47%
Skratowski – couple	CLY 1990 – 1543	£710.00	£355.00	50%	£1,250.00	176%
Maciak – couple	CLY 1992 – 1536	£4,290.00	£1,430.00	33%	£1,050.00	23.77%
Koncziak – family 3	CLY 1994 – 1474	£135.00	–	–	£300.00	222%
Suttill – family of 4	CLY 1994 – 1475	£2,550.00	£750.00	29%	£300.00	11.76%
Charles – family of 6	CLY 1994 – 1476	£1,223.40	£611.70	50%	£1,500.00	122.60%
Coles	CLY 1994 – 1477	unknown	–	–	£1,000.00	unknown
Wheelhouse	CLY 1994 – 1478	£2,548.00	£382.00	15%	£1,000.00	39.24%
Rebello – couple	CLY 1994 – 1601	£1,448.60	£650.00	44.87%	£450.00	31.06%
Clarke – family of 8	CLY 1995 – 1603	£2,058.25	£1,000.00	48.59%	£6,400.00	310.94%
Causby – couple	CLY 1995 – 1604	£602.00	–	–	£330.00	54.81%
Kelly – family of 5	CLY 1995 – 1605	£1,884.70	£950.00	50.40%	£1,850.00	98.15%
Parr – family of 3	CLY 1996 – Oct 131	£570.00	£570.00	100%	£1,250.00	219.29%
Richards – party of 64	CLY 1996 – Dec 150	unknown	£650.00	unknown	£650.00	unknown
Graham – couple(?)	CLY 1997 – Jan 246	£2,159.00	–	21.18	£1,000.00	46.31%
Morris – party of 5	CLY 1997 – Feb 215	£1,180.00	£250.00	253%	Nil	Nil
Lynes & Graham	CLY 1997 – June 193	£592.00	£1,500.00	50%	No separate award	–
Crump	CLY 1998 – Jan 156	£2,194.00	£1,097.00	50%	£1,250.00	60%
Collinson	CLY 1998 – Jan 157	£4,820.00	£1,300.00	26%	No separate award	–

HOLIDAY CLAIMS

Special damages

Special damages comprise either:

- out-of pocket expenses; or
- foreseeable consequential losses.

The variety of **out-of-pocket expenses** recoverable is almost infinite in theory. Table B, however, shows that in the reported cases the same categories of expense occur time and again. The most common are:

- the cost of meals taken outside poor hotel accommodation;
- the cost of meals incurred due to travel delays;
- car hire charges and parking;
- travel costs incurred as a result of change of accommodation;
- telephone calls.

In many of the reported cases, some of the incidental out-of-pocket expenses are implicitly included in the court's award of damages for loss of bargain. Occasionally, the loss of bargain element is described as "special damage" – particularly where it is calculated arithmetically as a proportion of the travel costs (*e.g. Wheelhouse* [1994] CLY 1428 15% of holiday cost included in "special damage").

Consequential losses are also recoverable. The loss of professional fees or wages can be recovered where a consumer takes time off work only to find that his travel arrangements are delayed or cancelled – *e.g. Taylor* [1984] CLY 1023.

Possible out-of-pocket expenses and consequential losses are included in the following Checklists.

Checklist 1

Out-of-pocket expenses

(Case references can be found in Table B)

- Alternative accommodation where provision is unsafe or manifestly inadequate.
- Alternative accommodation in the absence of any contractual provision.
- Cost of travel home where arrangements curtailed.
- Meals out due to poor hygiene or catering standards.
- Meals and food as a result of delays and cancellation.
- Entertainment that should have been free.
- Entertainment at greater cost than expected.
- Excursion or sightseeing costs where itinerary curtailed or free provision ignored.
- Taxis or alternative transport – where car hire not reasonable for additional travel.
- Cost of child care – *e.g.* where children's club not provided or unsatisfactory.
- Entertainment to compensate for poor accommodation or location.
- Car hire to mitigate poor location.
- Parking, tolls, insurance and petrol to mitigate poor location.
- Car hire, tolls, insurance and petrol to compensate for poor accommodation.
- Car repairs or servicing.
- Associated car costs – cleaning – maps – sunshields.
- Parking costs incurred at home due to delayed return; or alternative place of return or departure.
- Sports equipment hire in absence of free or safe provision.
- Equipment hire or purchase where private equipment delayed or lost in transit.
- Access costs (*e.g.* ski passes; fishing rights) in absence of free provision.
- Telephone, telex and communication charges.
- Clothes costs due to damage, loss or delay in transit or damage due to state of accommodation or other breaches of contract.
- Clothes cleaning.
- Cleaning materials for poor accommodation.

- Replacement bedding in the absence of proper provision.
- Cutlery and crockery in self-catering accommodation in absence of free provision.
- Medication.
- Cost of medical care.
- Expenses incurred in specialised circumstances – *e.g.* the cost of new wedding photographs; re-organised wedding; hire or purchase of flowers, clothes, food or entertainment where free provision is absent or where free provision unreasonably below contracted standard.

Sometimes by incurring modest expenses a consumer can mitigate the loss that would otherwise have arisen. For example, expenditure of a little time and money cleaning a grubby apartment might make the accommodation perfectly habitable. If this expenditure and the work involved falls within reasonable limits, the cost of time and materials may represent the limit of the consumer's entitlement to damages. A graphic example of this is a German case reported in *Neue Juristische Wochenschrift:* 13–95 where the purchase by the consumer of some string to tie together twin beds would have prevented the disruption to his sex life which was at the centre of his action against the tour operator for damages for failing to provide a double bed.

Checklist 2

Consequential losses – where foreseeable

- Loss of earnings due to delayed return travel.
- Loss of earnings for recuperation if necessary.
- Loss of earnings due to delayed departure (subject to proof that work would have been done).
- Additional transport costs (*e.g.* taxis, petrol, parking) caused by delayed return, or return to alternative destination.
- Costs associated with missed travel connections – flights – accommodation – meals.
- Costs associated with other leisure, social or family activities lost due to delays.
- On-going medical treatment and medication.
- Additional expenses incurred for home security or child care.

Table B

Case	Reference	Special damages awarded
Hunt – school trip – children.	CLY 1983 – 983	None
Hunt – teachers	CLY 1983 – 983	None
Hunt – lead teacher	CLY 1983 – 983	None
Rhodes – family of 5	CLY 1983 – 984	None
Taylor – family	CLY 1984 – 1023	Cost of travel to alternative airport Alternative parking 1 week's wages for unnecessary time off Loss of wife's fee for professional engagement she could have done but for breach by tour operator
Bagley -single	CLY 1984 – 1024	Hotel accommodation costs whilst awaiting deportation
Abbatt – family of 4	CLY 1984 – 1025	None
Scott – couple	CLY 1985 – 943	Cost of eating out of hotel where food was poor
Harris – family of 5	CLY 1985 – 944	Cost of eating out of poor hotel Cost of parking a hired car – free parking not available
Powell – couple	CLY 1985 – 945	None
Tucker – family of 3	CLY 1986 – 383	"Out of pocket expenses" – costs of telexes, petrol, food
Jacobs – family of 4	CLY 1986 – 975	Telephone calls and earnings lost during period of cancelled holiday
Carter – family of 5	CLY 1986 – 976	None
Glover – couple	CLY 1987 – 1151	Hiring diving equipment – theirs lost in transit. Unspecified sundries
McLeod – family	CLY 1987 – 1162	None
Duthie – single	CLY 1988 – 1058	Camp site fees and hotel costs where promised accommodation not provided
Wilson – school trip	CLY 1988 – 1059	None
Wilson – teacher	CLY 1988 – 1059	None

Case	Reference	Special damages awarded
Wilson – party leader	CLY 1988 – 1059	None
Jones – family	CLY 1988 – 1061	None
Graham – family	CLY 1989 – 1189	None
Corbett – couple	CLY 1989 – 1194	Cost of flight and taxi home – holiday abandoned
Booth – couple	CLY 1990 – 1542	None
Skratowski – couple	CLY 1990 – 1543	Cost of eating elsewhere
Maciak – couple	CLY 1992 – 1536	Cost of moving to alternative accommodation and ultimately flights home
Koncziak – family 3	CLY 1994 – 1474	Cost of extra meals in delayed coach trip
Suttill – family of 4	CLY 1994 – 1475	Cost of hiring a car
Charles – family of 6	CLY 1994 – 1476	Wasted hire car charges
Coles	CLY 1994 – 1477	Cost of food and entertainment that should have been covered by vouchers – hire car costs, extra accommodation and taxis
Wheelhouse – family	CLY 1994 – 1478	Alternative hotel; taxis
Rebello – couple	CLY 1995 – 1601	None
Clarke – family of 8	CLY 1995 – 1603	Eating out
Causby – couple	CLY 1995 – 1604	None
Kelly – family of 5	CLY 1995 – 1605	Unspecified expenses incurred as a result of families temporary displacement from hotel facilities by rowdy football hooligans
Parr – family of 3	CLY 1996 – Oct 131	Insurance refund; food; telephone calls; taxis; travel to alternative airport – all in vain to salvage a cancelled holiday
Richards – party of 64	CLY 1996 – Dec 150	Petrol & toll costs for extra vehicle taken to supplement inadequate coach
Graham – couple(?)	CLY 1997 – Jan 246	Given free hire car by tour operator & £200.00 to cover all extras

HOLIDAY CLAIMS

Mitigation – double recovery

Principle The consumer is only entitled to recover that which has actually been lost – whether by way of bargain, enjoyment or pecuniary expenses.

Double recovery

Where a consumer spends money which it is sought to recover as part of the pecuniary expenses (*e.g.* accommodation in appropriate alternative rooms) this expenditure should in most cases mitigate both the loss of bargain and loss of enjoyment damages. Clearly where alternative accommodation has been purchased the loss of enjoyment caused by the originally poor accommodation is lessened. Depending on location and facilities, loss of enjoyment may be limited to only that period of time it took to locate and move into the alternative rooms.

Chesnau v *Interholme* [1983] NLJ 341
Trackman v *New Vistas Ltd* [1959] *The Times*, 24 November.

If a holiday provider is paying in special damages for the cost of alternative accommodation, the loss of bargain suffered by the consumer may be eradicated altogether.

Usually, where the cost of suitable alternative arrangements are included and recovered, the elements of lost bargain and enjoyment will be *diminished* to the extent of this recovery. The same applies where a consumer unreasonably refuses to accept alternative arrangements made by the holiday provider, even though the alternative may not be precisely equivalent to the original facilities promised.

See *Czyzewski* v *Intasun* Grant & Mason (1990) page 238.

HOLIDAY CLAIMS

Limitation of and liquidated damages

Liability of tour operator or holiday provider

In non personal injury cases it is commonplace for holiday providers to impose limitations on the amount of damages they will pay in the event of "quality" complaints.

These limitations are designed to apply in two situations. The first (Table C) is where major or significant changes are made in the contract by the provider either before or after departure and the consumer elects either to proceed despite the change or accept an alternative comparative holiday. The scales of compensation imposed in these circumstances should be read in conjunction with *regulations 12, 13 and 14 of the Package Travel, Package Holidays and Package Tours Regulations* 1992. The second (Table D) situation is to address quality complaints by consumers on their return home.

As these scales of damages are frequently to be found in the operator's standard terms and conditions, to which the reasonableness provisions of the Unfair Contract Terms Act 1977 apply. Such limitations *cannot* be imposed on personal injury claims. Examples of such scaled limitations can be found in Tables C and D.

As an alternative to pre-set scales of damages tour operators sometimes limit their liability in "quality" complaint cases by reference to *maximum compensation* of (say) twice the price of the holiday – the "price" being the total cost to a group travelling on one Confirmation Invoice.

There is no reported case in which the scaled "quality" complaint damages have been successfully challenged.

Liability of consumer

If a consumer cancels the holiday arrangements liquidated damages are usually payable to the holiday provider on the basis of a scale set out in the "small print" of the brochure. A table of customary cancellation charges is also given in the following pages. The consumer's liability to pay such liquidated damages should be seen in the context of *regulation 10 of the 1992 Regulations* (the right to transfer the benefit of the holiday to a third party). An example of scaled compensation payable by the consumer is set out in Table E. A charge may be levied by the tour operator when the right to transfer is exercised by the consumer.

Table C

Suggested scales of compensation payable *to* consumer in the event of significant changes.

Period of notification prior to travel	Compensation per passenger
More than 56 days	Nil
43–56 days	£10.00
29–42 days	£20.00
15–28 days	£30.00
0–14 days	£40.00

Table D

Scales of damages [non personal injury cases] for quality complaints.

Nature of complaint	Compensation per passenger [maximum]
Minor complaint not compromising purpose of holiday	£25.00 per day
Minor complaint arising out of main purpose of holiday	£50.00 per day
Serious complaint concerning individual facilities but affecting whole holiday	£75.00 per day
Complaints where the entire holiday has been effectively ruined	£100.00 per day

But in any event, compensation in respect of complaints other than those involving personal injury or death will not exceed twice the total price of the holiday as set out on the Confirmation Invoice.

Table E

Compensation payable by the consumer in the event of cancellation.

Notice period of cancellation	Amount payable by consumer
More than 56 days	Deposit only
28–56 days	50% of invoice price
22–28 days	60% of invoice price
1–21 days	The whole price

HOLIDAY CLAIMS

Compensation under the Package Travel [etc] Regulations 1992

Sources   SI 1992 No 3288 – Appendix 1
Saggerson – *Travel Law & Litigation*

Most reported cases under the Regulations have been decided under regulation 15 according to the general principles set out in **Holiday Claims – an overview**. There are very few, if any, reported cases arising out of the secondary provisions of the Regulations which are illustrated below.

1 Regulation 4

"(1) No organiser or retailer shall supply to a consumer any descriptive matter concerning a package, the price of a package or any other conditions applying to the contract which contains any misleading information.

(2) If an organiser or retailer is in breach of paragraph 1 he shall be liable to compensate the consumer for any loss which the consumer suffers in consequence."

This is a wide ranging provision. It clearly applies to tour operators, but also extends to travel agents and could even extend to newspaper and magazine publishers and suppliers who are retailers of material which often carries descriptive matter concerning package holidays. In practice, it is unlikely that the section would ever be deployed other than against a tour operator or travel agent.

Descriptive matter includes but is not limited to brochures. It covers every imaginable type of promotional material, advertising and written or pictorial information. Oral statements are not included.

Misleading information includes, but is not limited to misrepresentations. The regulation also covers statements of opinion and future intention, and covers any description given about the country or resort destination as long as it *concerns* the package (*i.e.* the description does not have to be of a facility or service forming part of the package).

Any loss which the consumer suffers in consequence.

- Only consumers as defined by the Regulations can claim under regulation 4. Access to compensation is limited to those who have agreed to take a package or their agents (see reg 2(2)) and the consumer at large who suffers loss by relying on misleading information without taking a package cannot use this regulation to obtain compensation.
- The Regulations do not explain the nature of the recoverable losses. The words in regulation 4(2) must be given their ordinary meaning. *Any* loss suffered in consequence of the misleading information is recoverable.
- The loss that is suffered, therefore, need not be a loss that derives from a failure to provide a package service or facility, so regulation 4 has wider appeal than the standard case under regulation 15.

Illustrations Advertising material shows the front of a hotel apparently built on the edge of a promenade and overlooking the beach and sea. The photographer has been able to disguise the fact that between hotel and beach there is a busy dual carriageway. Elderly couple book a package holiday in the hotel relying on *inter alia* the photographic representation. They are injured when trying to cross the road to the beach.

Regulation 4 may justify an action against the tour operator and travel agent for disseminating the misleading material, reliance on which led the elderly couple to choose the "beach-side" hotel in consequence of which they faced the dangerous route across the road and suffered injury.

It may be possible for consumers to use regulation 4 in situations where illness or injury is caused by independent persons outside the scope of the package contract itself, where reliance has been placed on information of a general character set out in a brochure. For example, consumers who act on a eulogistic general descriptions of restaurants or night-life might succeed where they have suffered food poisoning, even though the restaurant in question was not providing package services.

Assessment   In the absence of any guidance in the Regulations it is thought that the assessment of the quantum of damages would follow general principles as described in **Holiday Claims – an overview**.

2 Regulation 13

Pre-departure changes – withdrawal or cancellation

This regulation applies where the organiser is constrained to make significant alterations to the package contract entitling the consumer to withdraw from the contract, or accept changes to it by way of substitute arrangements.

Regulation 13(3) provides:

"The consumer is entitled, if appropriate, to be compensated by the organiser for non-performance of the contract ..."

This compensation is *additional* to the consumer's right to:

- a refund of the price in the event of cancellation;
- a substitute package with suitable price adjustments if the new package is a cheaper one.

So, where a consumer is entitled to a full or partial refund under regulation 13(2), or opts for a substitute package, the consumer should still be compensated *if appropriate* for any loss of enjoyment and associated expenses arising out of the cancellation of the original contract. It will be appropriate to claim this additional compensation whenever a substitute of equivalent value cannot be supplied, or whenever the substitute package omits components included in the original.

Illustration   Consumers buy a package to China which includes a cruise through the Yangtse Gorges. The package is cancelled, and the consumer accepts a substitute package to China of the same duration substituting additional days in cities where the cruise should have come.

The consumer should be entitled to damages for the lost enjoyment of a significant element of the original package (the cruise), even though the substitute holiday was of similar duration and standard.

If the consumer opts to accept a refund under regulation 13(2), compensation for loss of enjoyment is still recoverable, though the amount recovered may depend on whether the consumer could reasonably have taken a substitute holiday, even if not of equal value.

The organiser is excused from paying compensation if the reason for the cancellation of the package is insufficient numbers (as long as the consumer was notified of this possibility before booking), or unusual and unforeseeable circumstances beyond the control of the organiser the consequences of which could not have been avoided even with the exercise of all due care.

An example of unusual and unforeseeable circumstances might be a natural disaster.

3 Regulation 14

Changes after departure

Where after departure, the organiser is not able to provide a significant proportion of the package services, suitable alternative arrangements must be made at no extra cost to the consumer and *where appropriate* the organiser should compensate the consumer. Compensation is also recoverable where the organiser cannot make appropriate alternative arrangements, and is obliged to return the consumer back to the place of departure.

Compensation *where appropriate* is additional to the consumer's right to have suitable alternative arrangements made at no extra cost.

Compensation is likely to be appropriate wherever an material element of the original package cannot be provided even though the alternative arrangements are of a similar standard.

Illustration Consumers are informed that they cannot be accommodated in Raj Palaces for the remainder of their holiday. Instead they are to be accommodated in 5-star joint-venture hotels of a higher standard.

Compensation may still be payable even though the alternative accommodation was of a higher standard because of the loss of the historical associations and atmosphere of the Raj Palaces. However, some allowance is likely to be made to the organiser for the fact that higher class (more comfortable?) accommodation was provided, which is some compensation in itself.

4 Regulation 15

Liability for the proper performance of the obligations under a package contract

Damages under this provision are calculated in the manner described in detail in **Holiday Claims – loss of bargain**.

However, in addition to this mainstream liability, compensation is payable to consumers where:

- The other party to the contract fails to render assistance to a consumer in difficulty, even though "the difficulty" does not arise out of the contract services or facilities.
- The other party to the contract's local representatives fail to respond promptly to consumer complaints about the performance of the contract - whether those complaints are justified or not.

(See regulation 15(6), (7), & (8)).

Unlike regulations 4, 13 and 14, these do not expressly state that compensation should be payable to consumers, but as the obligations are deemed to be implied terms of the package contract, any breach of such terms must sound in damages.

Illustration A consumer may be injured as a result of the actions of a third party who has nothing at all to do with the package services. Having been injured, the consumer may need the assistance of the local "rep" with travel arrangements, insurance claims, or for contacting relatives. If the local "rep" does nothing to help, the consumer will be entitled to compensation, even though no compensation for the original injury would be due under the main provisions of regulation 15 for non-performance of the holiday contract.

Limits on liability

Regulation 15(4) provides that a package contract may include a term limiting the amount of compensation payable in the case of damage *other than personal injury* which results from the non-performance or the improper performance of the package contract provided the limitation is not unreasonable.

What is *not unreasonable* is yet to be tested in the courts under these provisions.

Regulation 15(3) allows the other party to the contract to take advantage of any limit on damages provided for in international conventions. This *includes* claims for personal injury.

Part 2

Travel – General

NON-HOLIDAY TRAVEL CLAIMS

Principles ● In cases where leisure is not a significant component of the travel arrangements damages for *loss of enjoyment and disappointment* are not recoverable.

● Damages for physical *incovenience* and *discomfort* are recoverable as part of the traveller's loss of bargain and are, therefore, recoverable in carriage only cases – *Bailey* v *Bullock* [1950] 2 All ER 1167; *Hobbs* v *London & South Western Railway Co* [1875] 10 LRQB 111 (the inconvenience of walking five miles from Esher to Hampton Court in the middle of the night – £8.00).

● The rule of thumb is that breaches of mere contracts of *carriage* do not give rise to damages for loss of enjoyment, because the provision of enjoyment, relaxation, or freedom from anxiety or disappointment was not part of the contract – *Hayes* v *Dodd* [1990] 2 All ER 815. In *Lucas* v *Avro* [1994] CLY 1444 a passenger on a charter flight was denied compensation for loss of enjoyment where the contract was for "flights only".

● Cases where there is a leisure *element* known to the carriage provider *do* allow for the recovery of damages for loss of enjoyment, even if leisure may not have been the primary purpose of the contract, provided the leisure element was significant.

Examples i Where business and leisure services form part of the same package.

ii Where the carrier knows that the carriage contract forms part of the passengers' leisure arrangements.

Inconvenience and discomfort

This is the only basis for general damages in carriage contract cases.

There are no authoritative guidelines on the quantum of such general damages.

It is thought that any award under this head would take into account the price of the ticket, and that the award would be in proportion to that price. Other factors might be:

- the availability of alternative means of transport
- the availability of accommodation where necessary
- the comfort and suitability of the alternative transport and accommodation
- the time and place of the breach of contract (*e.g.* was it the middle of a winter's night, and many miles from the intended destination)
- the assistance rendered by the carrier in breach
- the physical characteristics, (age, infirmities or disabilities) of the passenger.

Consequential losses

These often arise where the passenger is obliged to take overnight accommodation, or arrange alternative (more expensive) transport to reach the intended destination. Losses have also been claimed arising out of cancelled business appointments and lost business opportunities arising out of breaches of a contract of carriage.

Compensation arising out of lost business appointments and opportunities was refused in *Hamlin v Great Northern Railway*, 1 H&N 408 where a salesman had been diverted to Grimsby for the night when he needed to be in Hull. The court considered these losses too remote. The availability of mobile telephones and faxes and other modern means of communication would suggest that it will only be very rare occasions when the contemporary passenger is unable to alert third parties to a delay of diversion and thus avoid the worst consequences of missed appointments.

As a general rule, a published timetable does not constitute a warranty that the advertised times will be met. So, where consequential loss in the form of additional expenses on accommodation or transport have been suffered, their recovery is invariably in cases where the passenger has been *diverted* rather than merely delayed.

Reasonable expenses

However, the cost of alternative transport, or accommodation should be recoverable as a result of *Hobbs* v *London & South Western Railway Co* (above) where although the Plaintiff was denied compensation for vexation and annoyance, the court approved in principle the proposition that the cost of alternative transport should be recoverable. This right of recovery is subject to the limits of reasonableness. The cost of a special train to carry a passenger to the seaside for a dinner engagement was disallowed in *Le Blanche* v *LNWR* [1876] 1 CPD 286.

HOTELS

Sources   Hotel Proprietors' Act 1956
Chitty on Contracts (1994) Sweet & Maxwell, Volume 2, paragraph 32-071 etc
Downes & Paton – *Law for the Travel Industry* (1991) Croner, page 9

Loss or damage to goods

This section concerns the strict liability of innkeepers as defined by the Hotel Proprietors Act 1956. It is not concerned with the general fault-based liabilities of hoteliers, under the Occupiers' Liability Acts for example, or the law of negligence where a customer has suffered loss or personal injury. This section is confined to the special liability of hoteliers and innkeepers under statute. For this strict liability to apply, the person, or corporation concerned must be an innkeeper as defined by the Act (section 1). A distinction is drawn between hotels (to which innkeepers liabilities attach, and private boarding houses or private hotels to which they do not). A hotel to which the Act applies (section 1(3)) is an establishment held out as offering food, drink and sleeping accommodation to any traveller who appears willing and able to pay a reasonable sum for such services.

1   At common law

At common law an innkeeper is strictly liable for the *loss* of guests property within the precincts of the inn. The liability attaches for the loss of goods without proof of negligence on the part of the innkeeper or his servants or agents. The liability is to the customer in respect of the value of the goods at the time of their loss.

Accordingly, the innkeeper is liable even for the unexplained loss of goods by a guest within the precincts of the inn. The precincts or *hospitium* of the inn includes all buildings attached to the inn, such as garages, and also includes walled courtyards.

"An innkeeper is commonly said to be an insurer of goods of the guest brought to the inn against loss ..." (*Winkworth v Raven* [1931] 1 KB at 657 per Swift J)

At common law this insurer's liability (subject to limited recognised defences) probably does not extend to *damage* to the goods – but total loss by destruction is within the innkeeper's strict liability.

"... we think the cases shew that there is a defect in the innkeeper, wherever there is a loss not arising from the Plaintiff's negligence, the act of God or the Queen's enemies." (Pollock CB *Morgan* v *Ravey* (1861) 6 H & N 265)

Common law strict liability cannot be excluded by agreement. "Innkeepers have never been allowed to contract out of the liability imposed on them by the custom of the realm." (*Williams* v *Linnitt* [1951] 1 KB at 585). From time to time statute has come to the assistance of innkeepers to limit their otherwise strict liability.

2   The Hotel Proprietors' Act 1956
By section 1(2) of this Act the innkeeper's liability is extended to *damaged* goods.

The strict liability regime in respect of both *loss* and *damage* is then somewhat modified. By section 2(1), the regime is limited to those instances where the customer has booked sleeping accommodation, and the loss or damage occurs during the period commencing midnight before and ending the midnight after the customer was a guest at the hotel.

The Act does not in any way affect a hotel's fault-based liabilities in, for example, negligence, or under the Occupiers' Liability Acts, or the Supply of Goods and Services Act 1982.

Strict liability for loss and damage to motor vehicles (or property inside a vehicle) and live animals and equipment such as harnesses is excluded by section 2(2) of the Act. Again this has no impact on a hotel's general fault-based liabilities.

Otherwise, the innkeeper is strictly liable for loss and damage to and the safety of all movables and money brought onto the premises by guests, subject to the defences outlined above and in *Morgan* v *Ravey*.

3   Statutory limit of strict liability

To this apparently onerous regime, there is a statutory limitation.

The relevant provision is section 2(3).

Subject to strict conditions an innkeeper can limit his liability:

i   in respect of any one article to £50.00;
ii   in respect of the articles of any guest to £100.00 in total.

To take advantage of this limitation of strict liability a Notice must be *conspicuously* displayed where it can *conveniently* be read by guests at or near the hotel reception desk. The Notice *must be in the statutory form.* Even unintentional errors or omissions will not be tolerated. The statutory form of notice is reproduced here.

Notice

LOSS OF OR DAMAGE TO GUESTS' PROPERTY

Under the Hotel Proprietors' Act 1956 a hotel proprietor may in certain circumstances be liable to make good any loss of or damage to a guest's property even though it was not due to any fault of the proprietor or the staff of the hotel.

This liability however–

a   extends only to the property of guests who have engaged sleeping accommodation at the hotel;
b   is limited to £50 for any one article and a total of £100 in the case of any one guest, except in the case of

property which has been deposited, or offered for deposit, for safe custody;

c does not cover motor cares or other vehicles of any kind or any property left in them, or horses or other live animals.

This notice does not constitute an admission either that the Act applies to this Hotel or that liability thereunder attaches to the proprietor of this hotel in any particular case.

---

4 Loss of statutory limit

The protection of the statutory limit on the recovery of damages is lost by the hotel or innkeeper if:

i the notice is not displayed or not conspicuously displayed at or near reception;
ii the property in question was lost or damaged through the default or neglect of the innkeeper;
iii the property was deposited with the innkeeper expressly for safe keeping;
iv the property was offered to the innkeeper for safe keeping, but the innkeeper refused to receive it.

The basis of these exceptions to a hotel's right to rely on the statutory limitations is set out in section 2(3) and proviso of the 1956 Act. Section 2 is set out in full below.

"Modifications of liabilities and rights of innkeepers as such

2.—(1) Without prejudice to any other liability incurred by him with respect to any property brought to the hotel, the proprietor of an hotel shall not be liable as an innkeeper to make good to any traveller any loss of or damage to such property except where—

    (a) at the time of the loss or damage sleeping accommodation at the hotel had been engaged for the traveller; and

    (b) the loss or damage occurred during the period commencing with the midnight immediately preceding, and ending with the midnight immediately following, a period for which the traveller was a guest at the hotel and entitled to use the accommodation so engaged.

(2) Without prejudice to any other liability or right of his with respect thereto, the proprietor of an hotel shall not as an innkeeper be liable to make good to any guest of his any loss of or damage to, or have any lien on, any vehicle or any property left therein, or any horse or other live animal or its harness or other equipment.

(3) Where the proprietor of an hotel is liable as an innkeeper to make good the loss of or any damage to property brought to the hotel, his liability to any one guest shall not exceed fifty pounds in respect of any one article, or one hundred pounds in the aggregate, except where—

    (a) the property was stolen, lost or damaged through the default, neglect or wilful act of the proprietor or some servant of his; or

    (b) the property was deposited by or on behalf of the guest expressly for safe custody with the proprietor or some servant of his authorised, or appearing to be authorised, for the purpose, and, if so required by the proprietor of that servant, in a container fastened or sealed by the depositor; or

    (c) at a time after the guest had arrived at the hotel, either the property in question was offered for deposit as aforesaid and the proprietor or his servant refused to receive it, or the guest or some other guest acting on his behalf wished so to offer the property in question but, through the default of the proprietor of a servant of his, was unable to do so:

Provided that the proprietor shall not be entitled to the protection of this subsection unless, at the time when the property in question was brought to the hotel, a copy of the notice set out in the Schedule to this Act printed in plain type was conspicuously displayed in a place where it could conveniently be read by his guests at or near the reception office or desk or, where there is no reception office or desk, at or near the main entrance to the hotel."

Part 3

Air, Rail and Sea

INTERNATIONAL CARRIAGE BY AIR

Sources   Carriage by Air Act 1960 – Schedule 1
Carriage By Air (Sterling Equivalents) Order 1996 SI 1996 No
244 (Appendix 2)
Denied Boarding Compensation – Council Directive 91/295

Limits of liability

Article 22 of the Warsaw Convention 1929 (as amended by
the Hague Protocol 1955) – Schedule 1 to the Carriage by Air
Act 1960 sets out the following limits of liability. The
current sterling equivalents of these limitations are printed
in italics.

Carriage of persons: 250,000 Francs [*£15,885.58*] – Article
22(1)
Hand baggage: 5,000 Francs [*£317.71*] – Article 22(3)
Registered baggage: 250 Francs per kilogramme [*£15.89 per
kilo*] – Article 22(2)(a)

Exceptions **i**   By special contract the carrier may agree to a higher (but
not a lower) limit in respect of damage to persons. There
are many special contracts imposed by national
governments, see *e.g.* the Montreal Agreement for
flights in and out of North America.
ii   A claim in respect of registered baggage may be outside
the limit if at the time the baggage is registered a
declaration of value is made to the carrier. In these
circumstances the limit is the value on the declaration
(for which carriage a supplementary charge can be
made).

Intentional and reckless damage

If it is proved that the loss or damage was caused by the
carrier or its servants in the course of their employment
intentionally, or *recklessly* with knowledge that damage

would probably result the general limits under the convention do not apply at all.

See Article 25 of Schedule 1, Carriage by Air Act 1960.
See *Goldman* v *Thai Airways International Ltd* [1983] 1 WLR 1186 – as to the meaning of "recklessness".

Incorrect documentation

The carrier cannot rely on the limits of liability where the ticketing or carriage documents (*e.g.* airway bills) are not provided by the carrier or do not comply with the Convention (see Art 3, 4 and 9).

What is damage?

Articles 17, 18 and 19.

a   Personal injury

"... damage sustained in the event of death or wounding of a passenger or any other bodily injury ... . If the accident ... took place ... on board the aircraft or in the course of any of the operations of embarking or disembarking."

- Damage covers more than financial loss – it includes damage of a "more intangible kind" such as the loss to young children of their deceased's mother's care. *Preston* v *Hunting Air Transport* [1956] 1 QB 454
- It does not include psychological injury. *Sidhu* v *British Airways* [1995] PIQR P427 at 429.
- It covers pain and suffering attendant upon physical injuries, loss of earnings, expenses and care costs.

b   Baggage

"... damage sustained in the event of destruction or loss of or damage to ... if the occurrence which caused the damage so sustained took place during the carriage by air."

In addition a passenger can recover for "damage occasioned by delay in the carriage by air of passengers, baggage or cargo." (Art 19).

Assessment The assessment of damages is undertaken according to the laws of the country whose courts are seised of the matter. In this jurisdiction it is thought that the maximum figures provided for by Article 22 provide an artificial cut-off. That is, awards falling naturally within the limits are *not* reduced by reference to the ceiling. A very wide band of cases will, therefore, be valued at just over £15,000.00.

Denied boarding compensation

This Directive establishes common minimum rules within the European Union where passengers are denied access to *scheduled* flights for which they have a *valid ticket* and *confirmed reservation.*

Air carriers are obliged to devise and implement procedures for dealing with over-booked scheduled flights which are consistent with these minimum requirements.

Passengers are entitled to make a choice between:

- a full refund of the ticket price;
- a re-routing to the final destination at the earliest opportunity;
- a re-routing at a later date to suit the passenger's convenience.

A passenger who accepts a seat in a lower standard of flight accommodation is entitled to be re-imbursed the difference in the cost of the tickets.

In addition – whatever choice is made, the passenger is entitled to compensation.

- for flights of up to 3,500 kilometres – 150 ECU or approximately £120.00;
- for flights of more than 3,500 kilometres – 300 ECU – approximately £240.00.

The amount of compensation is halved if the passenger is conveyed to his final destination within two hours of the scheduled arrival time, or four hours in the case of long-haul flights.

Compensation may be further limited by the price of the ticket which is a *ceiling* on the amount of compensation payable. Those travelling by discounted or reduced fares may be entitled to a reduced sum in compensation as a result.

In addition the carrier is obliged to pay to the passenger compensation for out of pocket expenses – such as telephone calls, faxes, refreshments and where necessary accommodation if an overnight stay is required.

The Directive requires that all passengers who are denied boarding, should be given an explanatory leaflet at the time they are denied.

A lesson from America

The Supreme Court of the United States has ruled that a policy of overbooking flights and "bumping" fare-paying passengers, constitutes malicious conduct to consumers, and has awarded $50,000.00 in punitive damages.

See *Ralph Nader* v *Allegheny Airlines* digested: [1996] TLJ 138.

NON-INTERNATIONAL CARRIAGE BY AIR

Carriage by Air Acts (Application of Provisions) Order 1967 SI 1967 No 1480

This Order applies the international conventions to non-international carriage in respect of the United Kingdom. The regime of the international conventions is generally applied to non-international air travel. For example, a carrier loses the right to rely on damage limitation provisions where the plaintiff proves that the damage was caused with intent, or recklessly.

The limits on damages expressed in the Order are set out in Special Drawing Rights (SDR). These are higher than the limits applicable in most cases of international travel. For death or personal injury the limit is 100,000 SDR. For loss, damage or delay to registered baggage the limit is 17 SDR per kilo. The sterling equivalent of the SDR is set out in the table at Appendix 1.

INTERNATIONAL CARRIAGE BY SEA

Sources   Athens Convention
London Convention
Merchant Shipping Act 1995 – section 183

Regime   The regime enacted by the Merchant Shipping Act 1995 and the Athens Convention (1974) is very similar to that imposed by the Warsaw Convention in respect for international carriage by air.

Financial limits of liability

The financial limits of liability are described in "units of account" in the Convention. In turn, these are the equivalent of Standard Drawing Rights. In sterling equivalents the position is as follows:

- Damages for death or personal injury – about £38,000.00
- Loss or damage to cabin baggage – about £140.00
- Damage to vehicles – £2,750.00.

The United Kingdom has exercised its right to increase these limits as follows:

- Death and personal injury – £95,000.00
- Baggage – £1,100.00
- Motor vehicles – £2,750.00.

Loss of limitations

A carrier loses the right to rely on the limitations provided by the Convention or by national law in circumstances similar to those that apply under the Warsaw Convention: *i.e.* recklessly or deliberately caused damage.

Disasters   The Merchant Shipping Act 1995 also brings into effect provisions for disaster funds or "limitation funds" by which a carrier can limit the total amount payable in respect of a single event or arising out of a single occasion. It is open to carriers to open funds calculated in accordance with the provisions of the London Convention and section 187 and Schedule 7 of the 1995 Act. The ceiling of liability in a case to which a disaster fund applies will be 25 million SDRs. Within this overall limit, the cap for individual events is calculated by multiplying the passenger capacity of the ship by 46,666 units of account, and the product is then multiplied by the sterling equivalent of the SDR.

The cap on a disaster fund calculated in this way is worth approximately £20 million today.

Passengers' claims are measured proportionately to the total available in the fund thus calculated.

The Merchant Shipping Act 1995 makes provision for the application of the international rules to non-international carriage by sea in the United Kingdom.

INTERNATIONAL CARRIAGE BY RAIL

Sources   International Transport Conventions Act 1983
COTIF (Convention Relative aux Transports Internationaux Ferroviaires)
Command Paper Cmnd 8535 (English text of COTIF)

Uniform rules

The Convention applies uniform rules regarding the liability of railways for death, personal injury or other bodily or mental harm to a passenger (travelling on international travel documents) arising out of an accident in the course of international travel by rail provided the accident arises out of the operation of the railway whilst the passenger is on board, or is entering or alighting from the train.

Liability extends to the loss of or damage to luggage, but not to claims arising out of transport delays. Any claim resulting from delayed rail travel must be adjudicated in accordance with the laws of the country where the delay occurred.

Financial limits of liability

- Death or personal injury – 70,000 units of account.
- Damage to or loss of hand baggage – 700 units of account
- Registered baggage – 34 units of account per kilogram [or 500 units per item] where the passenger can demonstrate the value of the goods lost or damaged or 10 units of account where the passenger cannot show the value of his loss
- A refund of the carriage cost of registered baggage must also be given.

Units of account

The unit of account is the *Special Drawing Right* ("SDR")

The SDR is defined by the International Monetary Fund and expressed in the national currencies of its members.

In England, judgments are given in sterling as converted from the SDR at the rate applicable on the date of the judgment.

Special Drawing Rights

A table of currency values against IMF Special Drawing Rights is set out in Appendix 1.

Assessment of damages

Within the limits set out above the assessment of damages in individual cases is conducted in accordance with the principles of the general law in the territory where the accident is litigated.

Limits on liability

A railway is exempted from liability in whole or in part where the damage has been caused by the passengers own behaviour or fault; or by the behaviour of a third party which could not be avoided and the consequences of which could not be prevented despite the exercise by the railway of all due care. The railway is also excused where the damage has been caused by circumstances unconnected with the operation of the railway which despite the exercise of due care could not be avoided, and the consequences of which could not have been prevented.

Limitation period

Injured passengers have three years from the date of the accident within which to commence proceedings against the railway.

DOMESTIC CARRIAGE BY RAIL

Source   The National Conditions of Carriage

Incorporation of terms

The National Conditions apply to all train companies which run domestic scheduled passenger services on the rail network in Great Britain, except London Underground. Copies of the National Conditions are available from the ORR (see Appendix 3).

Delays   Clauses 42–45 govern compensation for delay.

- Compensation for delay is paid in vouchers representing a discount on future rail travel.
- It is only payable where the reason for the delay is within the control of the train company, or a rail service company.
- Compensation only arises where the delay concerned exceeds one hour.
- Where reasonable the train companies agree to render assistance to stranded passengers and provide overnight accommodation.

Luggage
- By clause 49 of the National Conditions liability for loss, damage and delay to luggage is accepted for the value of the item up to a maximum of £1,000.00 per item.
- This liability arises only where the reason for the loss, damage or delay is the fault of the train company or a rail service company.
- Unclaimed luggage is deemed abandoned one month after it comes into the possession of the train company.

Refunds   Subject to an administrative charge, unused portions of tickets will be refunded by train companies, unless the reason for the refund is the cancellation or delay of the service for which the booking is made – in which case no administrative charge for the refund is levied.

Part 4

European Personal Injury Damages

EUROPEAN PERSONAL INJURY COMPENSATION

Key facts

Introduction A claim against a British based defendant is not always possible. Litigants may have to rely on the courts of other jurisdictions. The following *key facts* in respect of damages for personal injuries available in a few of the major European travel destinations are offered as an introduction to the Heads of Loss recoverable in some other European countries.

No separate entries are made in respect of the Republic of Ireland or Scotland both of which jurisdictions have their own systems and rules, but where the recovery and assessment of damages for personal injury would be reasonably familiar to the practitioner in England and Wales.

Sources Campbell – *International Personal Injury Compensation Sourcebook* (1996) Sweet & Maxwell
Association of Personal Injury Lawyers – *Compensation for Personal Injury in Europe*

EUROPEAN PERSONAL INJURY COMPENSATION

Austria

Solatium
Damages for pain and suffering. Usually awarded by way of a lump sum, but where the prognosis is not clear at the time of assessment the court has power to make awards similar to those found in cases where provisional damages are awarded in England and Wales, and periodical payments. These are, however, the exception. Conventionally, the courts award compensation on a *daily basis* for pain and suffering – often between about £50.00 per day for slight pain; £75.00 per day for moderate pain, and £100.00 for intense pain.

Disfigurement
Where a person's appearance has been changed by injuries, there is claim for disfigurement if it can be shown that the change has affected the victim's chances in life in some way. Diminished prospects of marriage (both men and women) is a common head of claim in this context. This is usually in the form of a lump sum, and in bad cases can be as much as approximately £120,000.

Loss of earnings – past and future
These are awarded by periodical payments in accordance with the actual losses sustained by the victim - up to the date of retirement. In the case of housewives, and those who have no earnings prior to an accident a notional figure is used to compensate the victim, known as an "abstract" periodic payment. This is seldom more than approximately £50.00 per month.

Fatal accidents
In general, the compensator must pay the equivalent of alimony to the family of the deceased. Payment is by way of pension or periodical payments.

General
- The limitation period is generally three years calculated from the date of the injured party's knowledge.
- Legal aid is available subject to means.
- Costs usually follow the event.

EUROPEAN PERSONAL INJURY COMPENSATION

Belgium

Moral damage

Damages similar to an award for pain, suffering and loss of amenity which extends to all physical and psychological suffering arising out of the accident including the claimant's reasonable perception that life is less enjoyable by reason of the accident even in the absence of continuing physical disability.

Aesthetic damage

Awards for aesthetic damages are in respect of scarring or other forms of disfigurement separate from the other aspects of physical and psychological suffering.

Material damage

Medical expenses and loss of earnings are included in this category. Loss of earnings includes prejudice on the labour market and compromised earning capacity as well as taking account of any extra effort required of the claimant in earning his living.

Fatal accidents

Damages for bereavement are recoverable but assessed on a case by case basis according to the factual as well as the familial relationship of the claimant to the deceased. A claim vests in the heirs of the deceased and includes financial losses actually incurred and likely to be incurred by the heirs as a result of the death.

General
- Each party pays their own costs.
- Legal aid is available but is subject to an application and hearing in open court at which the other side may be represented.

EUROPEAN PERSONAL INJURY COMPENSATION

Denmark

Damages in Denmark are governed by the Damages Liability Act which provides in tabulated form the maximum amounts recoverable for pain and suffering and for permanent disability. In addition, damages are recoverable for medical expenses, other consequential expenses and loss of earnings. The Danish system appears to be one of the most arithmetical approaches to personal injury damages assessment in Europe.

Pain and suffering

The compensator must indemnify the injured party by reference to the number of days the injured person is confined to bed, and the number of days of incapacity or illness where the injured party is not confined to bed. The amounts payable are adjusted on an annual basis. The *maximum* recoverable is approximately the equivalent of £2,000. In cases of permanent disability the maximum is approximately £32,000.

For claimants over 60, the amount of damages is reduced by 5% per annum for each year the age exceeds 59, up to a maximum of 50%.

For up to date figures the current tables must be referred to.

EUROPEAN PERSONAL INJURY COMPENSATION

Finland

Material injuries

- *Actual losses.* Those expenses and costs (including medical expenses) which have been caused by the accident.
- *Indirect losses.* Loss of earnings and future loss including the cost of care and rehabilitation expenses.

Non-material injuries

- Pain – often calculated on the basis of recommendations by the national traffic accident board.
- Physical harm and disability.
- Distress – where the injury is the result of a criminal act.

Future loss Future loss is compensated whether this arises out of compromised earning capacity or the future cost of care. Such awards can be reviewed in the light of future events and adjusted or rectified to meet a change of circumstances.

Dependants Claims are based on the amount required to maintain the dependant until he is able to support himself.

General Costs follow the event if they are specifically pleaded.

An impecunious claimant can apply for a "free trial".

The limitation period is generally 10 years – but special acts limit this period in certain cases. Where the claim is based on a criminal act the period will be 10 years or the equivalent of the criminal limitation period whichever is longer.

EUROPEAN PERSONAL INJURY COMPENSATION

France

Patrimonial (pecuniary)
- Medical and other expenses incurred by reason of the accident.
- Loss of earnings.
- Future loss of earnings and loss of earning capacity (net of social security contributions but not income tax).

Extrapatrimonial (moral damages)
- Pain and suffering.
- Loss of amenity.
- Cosmetic defect.
- Impaired enjoyment of life.
- Bereavement or suffering for the family due to death or disability of accident victim.

Dependants Awarded on a similar basis to that under the Fatal Accidents Act 1976 (as amended).

Evidence The courts frequently refer to tables produced by actuaries and other professional bodies in determining the extent of future losses.

General France has a criminal injuries compensation scheme which is available to foreigners.

The limitation period is 10 years from the date of the occurrence.

Legal aid is available to foreigners who habitually reside in France or where the country of residence of the victim is a signatory to the European Agreement on the Transmission of Applications for Legal Aid.

EUROPEAN PERSONAL INJURY COMPENSATION

Germany

Special costs

- Necessary medical expenses commensurate with the level of treatment the victim would have enjoyed if he had paid for it himself – but subject to a deduction representing any savings made as a result of not living at home.
- Necessary costs of relatives and visitors.
- Incidental costs, similar to special damages including the cost of the victim's "increased needs".

Occupational losses

- Loss of income or profits.
- Future loss of earnings. This is often ordered in the form of a monthly pension, a scheme which also covers the cost of the claimant's increased needs.

Pain and suffering

- Damages under this head are awarded – but as an exception to the general principle of German law that only damage to property is subject to compensation.
- Such damages include a punitive element – recklessness or intentional damage will increase the award in many cases to give *satisfaction* to the injured party.

Fatal accidents

- Funeral expenses.
- Alimony – similar to a claim for dependancy.

General

The limitation period is usually three years from the claimant's date of knowledge with a long-stop of 30 years in any event.

Costs are dealt with by established pre-negotiated schedules – similar to fixed rate scales.

EUROPEAN PERSONAL INJURY COMPENSATION

Greece

Damage to body and health

- Direct harm to the human body in which disfigurement or disability are given special weight.
- Any deterioration of the human physical or mental functions.
- All expenses incurred in restoring the claimant to health.

Future deprivation

- Nursing and care expenses for the victim or his dependants.
- Loss of earnings and loss of future earnings or profits.
- Future losses are often ordered to be paid in monthly installments. Lump sums are ordered only in exceptional cases.

Third party claims

A third party economically damaged by the injury to the claimant can make a separate claim.

Fatal accidents

- Dependants of a deceased accident victim are compensated by *maintenance payments* usually monthly according to the amount that the deceased would have been obliged to pay by law.
- Loss of services of the deceased.

General

There is no meaningful provision for legal aid.

Costs do not always follow the event.

The limitation period is five years from the date of the claimant's knowledge with a long-stop of 20 years.

EUROPEAN PERSONAL INJURY COMPENSATION

Italy

Physical damage

Damages for permanent or temporary detriment to the health of the injured party and the ability to enjoy life.

Pecuniary damage

Expenses incurred as a result of the accident and accrued loss of earnings at the date of any trial. Also, future losses, such as anticipated losses of earnings in the event of permanent injury.

Moral damage

A form of aggravated damages following injury by criminal activity.

Commentators regard the Italian system of compensation as unpredictable and inordinately lengthy. (*e.g.* de Miro – *International Personal Injury Sourcebook*).

General   In road accident cases there is a direct right of action against the insurer of the party causing the accident.

The limitation period is generally five years from the date of the injury, but in road traffic cases the period is two years from the date of the accident.

If a personal injury claim is brought in contract (*e.g.* as a result of an accident in a taxi, or resulting from some leisure activity) once the injury is established as a consequence of the event, the defendant bears the burden of proving that all due care had been exercised to avoid such incidents.

EUROPEAN PERSONAL INJURY COMPENSATION

Netherlands

Non-pecuniary damage

- Covers pain and loss of amenity taking into factors familiar to those assessing damages in English law.
- *e.g.* age, occupation of the victim; disabilities; nature and extent of remaining symptoms; degree and duration of pain; impact on working capacity and marriage prospects.

Recovery costs

- This includes the cost of medical treatment.
- Also the cost of "essentials" such as drugs.
- Transport costs for medical treatment.
- Special needs costs for nutrition, care and additional housekeeping.

Pecuniary losses

- Legal costs and the cost of assessing damages is included in the claim.
- Incidental costs following the injury – an example awarded in the Netherlands would the be the reasonable cost of holiday to recover from the effects of the accident.
- Future costs of mobility aids (including modified motor vehicles) and housekeeping assistance.
- Loss and future loss of earnings – including loss of earning capacity.

Third parties Third parties may claim visiting costs, and the cost of looking after an injured person as well as any expenses outlined above that the third party has incurred rather than the injured party.

General   Each party pays their own costs – but costs can be claimed as part of the pecuniary losses. The court awards such costs as damages, but on the basis of predetermined scales. The full costs are seldom recovered.

Generous provision is made for legal aid.

EUROPEAN PERSONAL INJURY COMPENSATION

Spain

General   "Quantifying damages for personal injury ... is an extremely difficult task. The courts have absolute freedom to determine the damages payable in any particular case, and there can be wide disparities between the amounts awarded is similar cases in different areas of the country."

Campbell – *International Personal Injury Compensation* (1996) Sweet & Maxwell

Non-Financial Losses (danos no patrimoniales)

This covers damages for pain, suffering and disfigurement.

There has been some effort at the standardisation of awards for injuries caused by some types of accidents. Notably, in road accident cases there are non-binding schedules produced by the government to which the courts may make reference in assessing non-financial loss. However, the tables state that there is no reason why they should not be referred to in non-road accident cases. The tables should be viewed as being similar to the guidance produced by the Judicial Studies Board in England and Wales, though the tables are probably less influential. The tables award points to certain types of injuries against which the points are measured in pesetas. However the value of the point varies with the age category of the claimant and further adjustments are made taking account of the individual characteristics of the claimant (such as level of earnings). The maximum possible number of points is 100.

Example   The amputation of a foot is worth 30 points.
If the claimant is 30 years old a point is worth approximately £225.00.

The headline figure in damages would, therefore, be about £6,750.00.

If the claimant earns more than Ps 6m per annum, the award can be increased by 50%.
(The increase is up to 25% if earnings are between Ps 3m and 6m).

The final award could, therefore, be as much as £10,125.00 subject to further correction factors such as contributory fault or pre-existing disability.

Fatal accidents

There are separate tables for fatal accidents. Once again the non-pecuniary damages can increase the *higher* the income of the deceased.

Pecuniary losses (danos patrimoniales)

- Loss of earnings, both past and future are awarded on a basis that would be familiar in England and Wales.
- Reasonable medical expenses, past and future are also recoverable.

Costs   The losing party is likely to be ordered to pay the costs of an action.

EUROPEAN PERSONAL INJURY COMPENSATION

Switzerland

Satisfaction "Satisfaction" payments are the equivalent of damages for pain, suffering and loss of amenity, but the recovery of such a sum is usually restricted in Switzerland to cases of *permanent disability or disfigurement*. An award would include an impairment on the enjoyment of life and reduced life expectation.

If the injury is not considered to be one of some severity it is unlikely that any "satisfaction" award would be made. In any event Swiss awards are, by reputation, on the low side when compared to awards for general damages in England and Wales.

The Swiss system jealously oversees the proved *actual* losses of a claimant which may explain why there seems to be some reluctance to award damages for pain and suffering save in cases of permanent disability. This is because of the difficulties perceived with the objective measurement of such awards and a feeling that they are arbitrary.

Material loss

The Swiss courts will compensate for loss of earnings both accrued and future on what is described as the "concrete" basis - that is, according to the evidence produced in respect of any past or prospective losses. However, the amount recovered can be *reduced* (but never increased) according to the level of fault on the part of the perpetrator. A small degree of fault can reduce the award payable. A great degree of fault, however, will lead to punitive damages in any form.

All benefits payable to the claimant are recovered from the tortfeasor and taken into account in assessing the claimant's actual losses.

Damages can be awarded either by way of capitalised lump sum, or periodic payments, or a combination of both at the election of the claimant.

The expenses (medical or otherwise) incurred by an injured party are also recoverable in full.

General
- The limitation period is short – can be as short as 12 months from the date of knowledge.
- If the liability is uninsured, the tortfeasor can obtain a reduction in the award if it can be established that he will suffer hardship as a result.

Part 5

Appendices

Appendix 1 International Monetary Fund Treasurer's Department Currency Values in Terms of Special Drawing Rights (SDRs)

5 February 1998		Currency units per SDR		SDR per currency unit	
		02/05/98	02/04/98	02/05/98	02/04/98
Deutsche mark	DM	2.441760	2.455960	0.409543000	0.407173000
French francs	F	8.178860	8.213010	0.122267000	0.121759000
Japanese yen	Y	168.882000	169.739000	0.005921300	0.005891410
Pounds sterling	LST	0.822437	0.820348	1.215900000	1.219000000
US dollars	US$	1.360310	1.352180	0.735129000	0.739549000
Argentine pesos	ARG$	1.359630	1.351500	0.735497000	0.739919000
Australian dollars	$A	2.005170	1.987920	0.498712000	0.503041000
Austrian schillings	S	17.195700	17.290300	0.058154300	0.057836000
Bahrain dinars	BD	0.511477	0.508420	1.955130000	1.966890000
Bangladesh taka	TK	62.982400	62.605900	0.015877500	0.015973000
Belgian francs	BF	50.460700	50.706800	0.019817500	0.019721300
Brazilian reals	R$	...	1.519310	...	0.658196000
Canadian dollars	CAN$	1.957620	1.956740	0.510826000	0.511056000
Colombian pesos	COL$	1830.240000	1818.700000	0.000546377	0.000549846
Danish kroner	DKR	9.314720	9.365870	0.107357000	0.106771000
Finnish markkaa	FMK	7.414640	7.441590	0.134869000	0.134380000
Greek drachmas	DR	387.158000	388.617000	0.002582930	0.002573240
Icelandic kronur	ISK	...	98.384600	...	0.010164200
Indian rupees	RS	52.712000	52.248200	0.018971100	0.019139500
Indonesian rupiah	RP	...	...	...	...
Iranian rials	IRL$	2369.700000	2364.120000	0.000421996	0.000422992
Iraqi dinars	ID	0.422862	0.420335	2.364840000	2.379060000
Irish pounds	LIR	0.969641	0.972512	1.031310000	1.028270000

		Currency units per SDR		SDR per currency unit	
		02/05/98	02/04/98	02/05/98	02/04/98
Italian lire	LIT	2410.010000	2419.430000	0.000414938	0.000413322
Korean won	W	2176.500000	2118.730000	0.000459456	0.000471982
Kuwaiti dinars	KD	0.414051	0.412374	2.415170000	2.424990000
Libyan dinars	LD	0.525000	0.525000	1.904760000	1.904760000
Malaysian ringgit	M	...	...	...	...
Maltese liri	LMT	...	...	...	...
Nepalese rupees	NRS	84.747300	84.240800	0.011799800	0.011870800
Netherlands guilders	NLG	2.751640	2.762230	0.363421000	0.362027000
New Zealand dollars	NZ	2.313450	2.307470	0.432256000	0.433376000
Norwegian kroner	NKR	10.188000	10.194800	0.098154600	0.098089900
Omani rials	RO	0.523039	0.519913	1.911910000	1.923400000
Pakistan rupees	PRS	60.071600	59.712500	0.016646900	0.026747000
Portuguese escudos	ESC	249.971000	251.339000	0.004000480	0.003978700
Qatar riyals	QR	4.951530	4.921940	0.201959000	0.203173000
Saudi Arabian riyals	SRLS	5.094360	5.063910	0.196296000	0.197476000
Singapore dollars	S$	2.288040	2.273150	0.437056000	0.439920000
South African rand	R	6.677080	6.653400	0.149767000	0.150300000
Spanish pesetas	PTAS	...	207.681000	...	0.004815090
Sri Lanka rupees	SLRS	...	...	...	...
Swedish kronor	SKR	10.951900	10.907400	0.091309000	0.091681500
Swiss francs	SWF	1.969320	1.974860	0.507791000	0.506367000
Thai baht	TB	...	65.083100	...	0.015365000
Trin & Tobago dollars	TT$	8.548600	8.498720	0.116979000	0.117665000
UAE dirhams	UAED	4.993700	4.963850	0.200253000	0.201457000
Venezuelan bolivares	BS	...	692.992000	...	0.001443020

Appendix 2 The Carriage by Air (Sterling Equivalents) Order 1996 (SI 1996 No 244)

The Secretary of State for Transport, in exercise of the powers conferred by section 4(4) of the Carriage by Air Act 1961 (c27) and by that provision as applied by article 6 of the Carriage by Air Acts (Application of Provisions) Order 1967 (SI 1967 No 480 to which there are amendments not relevant to this Order) and now vested in him (SI 1966 No 741 and SI 1970 No 1537) and of all other powers enabling him in that behalf, hereby makes the following Order:

1. This Order may be cited as the Carriage by Air (Sterling Equivalents) Order 1996 and shall come into force on 29th February 1996.

2. The Carriage by Air (Sterling Equivalents) Order 1986 (SI 1986 No 1778) is hereby revoked.

3. The amounts shown in column 2 of the following Table are hereby specified as amounts to be taken, for the purposes of article 22 in the First Schedule to the Carriage by Air Act 1961 and that article as applied by article 5 of the Carriage by Air Acts (Application of Provisions) Order 1967 as equivalent to the sums respectively expressed in francs in column 1 of that Table:

Table

Column 1 Amount in francs	Column 2 Sterling equivalent
250	15.89
5,000	317.71
125,000	7,942.79
250,000	15,885.58

Signed by authority of the
Secretary of State fro Transport

Goschen
Parliamentary Under Secretary of State,
Department of Transport

6 February 1996

Explanatory note
(This note is not part of the Order)

This Order specifies the sterling equivalents of amounts, expressed in gold francs as the limit of the air carrier's liability under the Warsaw Convention of 1929, and under that Convention as amended by the Hague Protocol of 1955, as well as under corresponding provisions applying to international carriage by air to which the Convention and Protocol do not apply. It supersedes the Carriage by Air (Sterling Equivalents) Order 1986.

The sterling equivalents have been calculated by reference to the Special Drawing Right (SDR) value of a gold franc converted into sterling at the average market rate for the month ending 25 January 1996. The new sterling figures are approximately 16.53 per cent greater than those in the superseded Order. The SDR is based on a basket of 5 major world currencies.

Appendix 3 Useful Contacts

ABTA
68-71 Newman Street
London W1P 4AH
0171-637-2444

Air Transport Users Council
5th Floor,
Kingsway House
Kingsway
London WC2B 6QX

Civil Aviation Authority
CAA House
45-49 Kingsway
London WC2B 4AX

Consumers Association Limited
PO Box 9432
London NW1 4WA
2 Marylebone Road
London NW1 4DF

Department of Trade & Industry
Ashdown House
123 Victoria Street
London SW1E 6RB

IATA
Imperial House
15-19 Kingsway
London WC2B 6UN

International Travel Law Journal
Travel Law Centre
University of Northumbria at Newcastle
Newcastle Upon Tyne. NE1 8ST

Office of Fair Trading
15-25 Breams Buildings
London EC4A 1PR

Office of the Rail Regulator
1 Waterhouse Square
Holborn Bars
138 Holborn
London EC1N 2ST

Prisoners Abroad
72-78 Rosebery Avenue
London EC1R 4RR

Ski Club of Great Britain
118 Eaton Square
London SW1W 9ARF

Appendix 4 A Rough and Ready Reckoner

Some international currencies: value against the pound sterling
March 1998

This table of currency comparisons is intended as a rough and ready guide for ease of reference. Exchange rates change daily, and sometimes dramatically. The following comparisons should not be used other than as a quick guide.

Exchange rate per pound sterling

Austrian Schilling – 21

Belgian Franc – 62

Canadian Dollar – 2.31

Cypriot Pound – 0.875

Danish Kroner – 11.25

ECU – 1.5

Egyptian Pound – 5.6

Finnish Markka – 9.08

French Franc – 10.00

German Deutschmark – 2.99

Greek Drachma – 474

Hong Kong Dollar – 12.66

Indian Rupee – 65

Irish Punt – 1.20

Israeli Shekel – 5.86

Italian Lira – 2,950.00

Japanese Yen – 209.64

Exchange rate per pound sterling

Malaysian Ringgit – 6.56

Malta Lira – 0.65

Mexican Peso – 14.00

Netherlands Guilder – 3.37

New Zealand Dollar – 2.82

Norwegian Kroner – 12.44

Portuguese Escudos – 305.56

Singapore Dollar – 2.66

South African Rand – 8.14

Spanish Peseta – 253.49

Swedish Kroner – 13.12

Swiss Franc – 2.44

Thai Baht – 71.47

Tiunisian Dinar – 1.92

Turkish Lira – 383,356.00

US Dollar – 1.63

INDEX